MAR 16

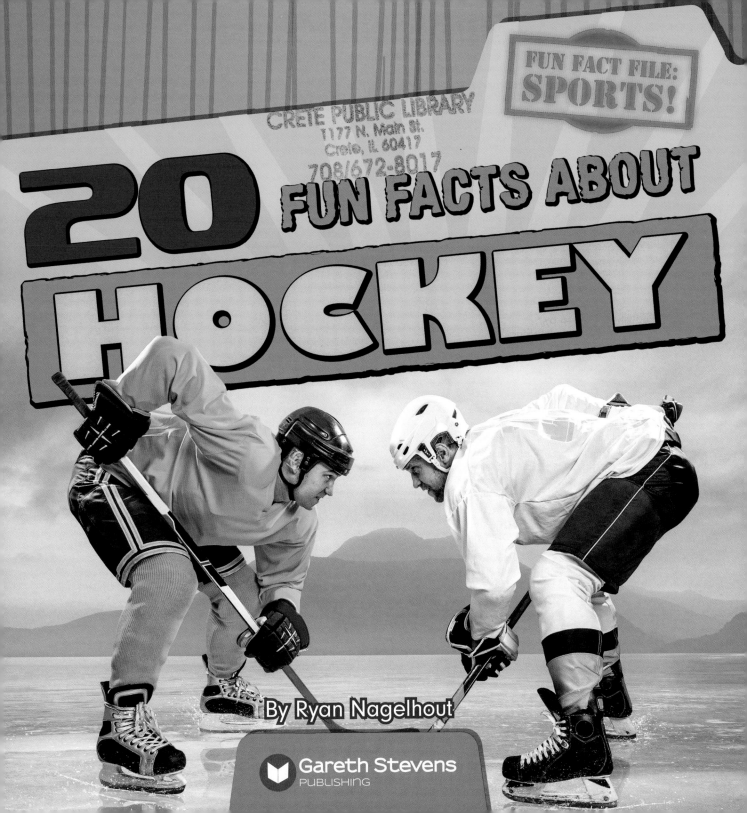

FUN FACT FILE: SPORTS!

20 FUN FACTS ABOUT HOCKEY

By Ryan Nagelhout

Gareth Stevens
PUBLISHING

Please visit our website, www.garethstevens.com. For a free color catalog of all our high-quality books, call toll free 1-800-542-2595 or fax 1-877-542-2596.

Library of Congress Cataloging-in-Publication Data

Nagelhout, Ryan.
 20 fun facts about hockey / Ryan Nagelhout.
     pages cm. — (Fun fact file: Sports!)
 Includes index.
 ISBN 978-1-4824-3978-6 (pbk.)
 ISBN 978-1-4824-3979-3 (6 pack)
 ISBN 978-1-4824-3980-9 (library binding)
 1. Hockey—Miscellanea—Juvenile literature. I. Title. II. Title: Twenty fun facts about hockey.
 GV847.25.N38 2016
 796.962—dc23

                                        2015030539

First Edition

Published in 2016 by
Gareth Stevens Publishing
111 East 14th Street, Suite 349
New York, NY 10003

Copyright © 2016 Gareth Stevens Publishing

Designer: Sarah Liddell
Editor: Ryan Nagelhout

Photo credits: Cover, p. 1 Andrey Yurlov/Shutterstock.com; p. 5 Pictorial Parade/Staff/Archive Photos/Getty Images; p. 6 Voyager/Wikimedia Commons; p. 7 Sports Illustrated/Contributor/Sports Illustrated/Getty Images; p. 8 OZaiachin/Shutterstock.com; p. 9 Andy Devlin/Contributor/National Hockey League/Getty Images; p. 10 B Wippert/Contributor/Bruce Bennett/Getty Images; p. 11 Bill Smith/Contributor/National Hockey League/Getty Images; p. 12 Jeff Vinnick/Contributor/National Hockey League/Getty Images; p. 13 (flag) RabidBadger/Shutterstock.com; p. 13 (jersey) Len Redkoles/Contributor/National Hockey League/Getty Images; pp. 14, 20 B Bennett/Contributor/Bruce Bennett/Getty Images; p. 15 John Iacono/Contributor/Sports Illustrated/Getty Images; p. 16 David E. Klutho/Contributor/Sports Illustrated/Getty Images; p. 17 Sporting News Archive/Contributor/Sporting News/Getty Images; p. 18 Denis Brodeur/Contributor/National Hockey League/Getty Images; p. 19 Christian Petersen/Staff/Getty Images Sport/Getty Images; p. 21 Jim McIsaac/Staff/Getty Images Sport/Getty Images; p. 22 Steve Babineau/Contributor/National Hockey League/Getty Images; p. 23 Alaney2k/Wikimedia Commons; p. 24 UniversalImagesGroup/Contributor/Getty Images; p. 25 Jonathan Daniel/Staff/Getty Images Sport/Getty Images; p. 26 Bruce Bennett/Staff/Getty Images Sport/Getty Images; p. 27 S Levy/Contributor/Bruce Bennett/Getty Images; p. 29 Noah Graham/Contributor/National Hockey League/Getty Images.

Printed in the United States of America

CPSIA compliance information: Batch #CW16GS: For further information contact Gareth Stevens, New York, New York at 1-800-542-2595.

Contents

Words in the glossary appear in **bold** type the first time they are used in the text.

Hockey History

It's easy to see why hockey was once called the coolest game on Earth. You might play roller or floor hockey with your friends, but the game was originally played on **frozen** ponds and indoor ice rinks. Hockey is fast, fun, and full of interesting facts.

Big shots and even bigger saves highlight a game filled with heroes known as "The Great One" and "The Dominator." Let's lace up our skates and take a shot at some of hockey's wackiest history.

Maurice Richard

Hockey has some of the most fun nicknames in sports. Did you know Montreal's Maurice Richard was called the "Rocket" when he hit the ice?

Puck Points

FACT 1

The first hockey pucks were frozen cow poo!

The first hockey games were played on ponds outside with whatever could be found. Some other early hockey pucks were made by gluing two pieces of rubber together. These pucks would often split in half when they hit the goalpost!

Hockey pucks are actually frozen before a National Hockey League (NHL) game to help keep them from bouncing on the ice. About a dozen different pucks are used per game.

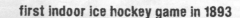
first indoor ice hockey game in 1893

FACT 2

The hockey puck has a birthday!

The word "puck" was used for the first time on February 7, 1876, in an article in the *Montreal Gazette*. The first pucks were the middle section of lacrosse balls that had been cut into thirds. Today's pucks are made out of **vulcanized** rubber.

FACT 3

Hockey sticks used to be called "twigs."

The first hockey sticks were made of wood pieces glued together, but today's sticks are made of **composite** materials, or matter. These materials are strong, but bend and twist easily, which lets players shoot harder.

Old hockey sticks also didn't have curved blades. The curve helps players lift pucks off the ice when they shoot.

composite stick   wooden stick

Hockey sticks are supposed to bend, but not break.

Sticks are measured by their flex, or the ability to bend when pressure is put on them. On a hard slap shot, the stick hits the ice behind the puck, which lets the stick flex and add more power to the shot.

Composite sticks often break more easily than old wooden sticks. A small crack in a stick can lead to a big break when a hard shot is taken.

Fun at the Rink

Until 1996, not every NHL rink was the same size!

A standard NHL ice rink is an oval 200 feet (61 m) long and 85 feet (26 m) wide. But not all old rinks were that size. Boston Garden, where the Bruins once played, was 191 feet by 83 feet (58 m by 25 m)!

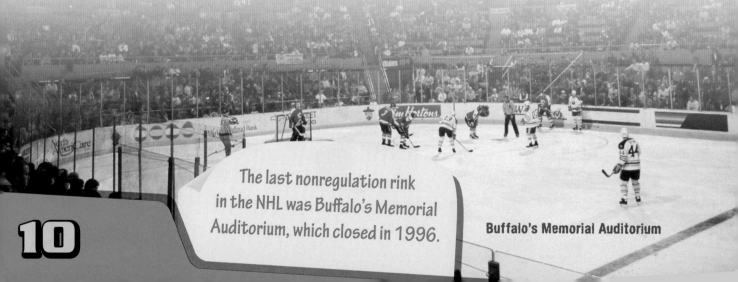

The last nonregulation rink in the NHL was Buffalo's Memorial Auditorium, which closed in 1996.

Buffalo's Memorial Auditorium

Fans carried the old **tradition** over from Chicago Stadium to the modern arena built on Madison Avenue in Chicago in 1994. It gets very loud in there during the playoffs!

FACT 6

Fans in Chicago cheer right through the national anthem at the "Madhouse on Madison."

During the 1985 Stanley Cup Finals, fans in Edmonton, Alberta, made some noise during "The Star-Spangled Banner." Chicago fans responded by cheering loudly while the organ played the song before Game 3. Chicago won the game, and now fans cheer through it at every home game.

Oh, Canada

FACT 7

Two Canadian NHL teams are named after...Canadiens.

The Montreal Canadiens are sometimes called the "Habs," thought to be short for "Les Habitants." That's a French term for the early French settlers in present-day Québec. The Vancouver Canucks joined the NHL in 1970. "Canuck" is a slang term for a person from Canada!

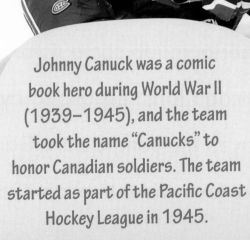

Johnny Canuck was a comic book hero during World War II (1939–1945), and the team took the name "Canucks" to honor Canadian soldiers. The team started as part of the Pacific Coast Hockey League in 1945.

The leaf on Canada's flag has 11 points on it, while Toronto's jerseys have featured leaves with different numbers of points.

Canadian flag

TORONTO MAPLE LEAFS

FACT 8

The Toronto Maple Leafs logo is much older than the maple leaf on Canada's flag.

Once called the Saint Pats, Toronto's team first had a green leaf on their jerseys in 1926. They changed it to blue and white the next season. Canada didn't have its own flag until 1965!

Great Gretzky

FACT 9

Wayne Gretzky first played pro hockey for the Indianapolis Racers!

Wayne Gretzky in 1978

In 1978, "The Great One" was signed by Indianapolis in the Western Hockey **Association** (WHA). Eight games into the season, he was traded to the Edmonton Oilers, who joined the NHL the following season when the WHA folded.

Gretzky is known for playing with the Oilers, the Los Angeles Kings, and the New York Rangers, but he also played for the St. Louis Blues in 1996!

14

Gretzky holds dozens of scoring records many believe will never be broken. In 1981, he scored 50 goals in his first 39 games!

Wayne Gretzky

FACT 10

Gretzky has more career assists than any other player has total career points!

Gretzky is first all-time in goals (894), assists (1,963), and points (2,857) in NHL history. Former teammate Mark Messier is second all-time in points, with "only" 1,887. Gretzky also holds the record for most goals (92), assists (163), and points (215) in a season.

Heroic Hasek

FACT 11

Dominik "The Dominator" Hasek dominated between the pipes.

As a Buffalo Sabre in the 1996–1997 and 1997–1998 seasons, Hasek won the Vezina **Trophy** for best goaltender, the Hart Memorial Trophy as the league's most valuable player (MVP), and the Lester B. Pearson Award for the player voted most outstanding by other players. He later won two Stanley Cups with the Detroit Red Wings, in 2002 and 2008.

Dominik Hasek

Hasek made amazing diving saves and shocked players with his flexibility. Some people said he had a spring for a spine!

Hasek's Highlights

WON HART MEMORIAL TROPHY 2 TIMES FOR LEAGUE MVP

WON VEZINA TROPHY 6 TIMES FOR BEST GOALTENDER

WON PEARSON AWARD 2 TIMES FOR PLAYERS' MVP

LED LEAGUE IN SHUTOUTS 4 TIMES

WON JENNINGS TROPHY 3 TIMES FOR FEWEST GOALS ALLOWED

LED LEAGUE IN SAVE PERCENTAGE FOR 6 STRAIGHT SEASONS

PLAYED IN 6 ALL-STAR GAMES

Family Time

FACT 12

Gordie Howe once played on a team with his sons!

"Mr. Hockey" played 32 pro seasons, including 25 with the Detroit Red Wings. In 1973—2 years after **retiring**—he signed with the WHA's Houston Aeros along with his sons, Marty and Mark. The 45-year-old Howe won league MVP, and Mark was named Rookie of the Year!

Mark played wing on Gordie's line, and the three Howes led Houston to WHA championships in 1974 and 1975.

Gordie   Marty   Mark

LA Kings coach Darryl Sutter

The NHL is full of Sutter brothers—and their sons.

Six brothers—Brent, Brian, Darryl, Duane, Rich, and Ron—have all spent time in the NHL, winning championships as players and coaches. Three of the Sutter brothers' sons—Brandon, Brett, and Brody—have also played in the NHL, and Lukas Sutter was drafted by the Islanders in 2014.

Islander Idols

FACT 14

The New York Islanders won four straight Stanley Cups from 1980 to 1983.

The Islanders joined the NHL as an **expansion team** in the 1972–1973 season. Seven years later, they won their first Stanley Cup. Seven people from those teams—including head coach Al Arbour—are members of the Hockey Hall of Fame.

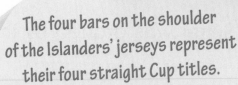

The four bars on the shoulder of the Islanders' jerseys represent their four straight Cup titles.

20

Arbour came out of retirement to coach his 1,500th game with the Islanders.

In 2007, Arbour signed a 1-day contract to come back and coach the team against the Pittsburgh Penguins. Arbour first retired in 1994. His 1,500 games coached are the most with a single team in NHL history.

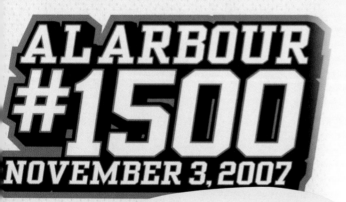

AL ARBOUR
#1500
NOVEMBER 3, 2007

Islanders coach Ted Nolan asked Arbour to come back and get his 1,500th game with the Islanders. The team raised a banner to celebrate his coaching total after the game.

FACT 16

A player once killed a bat during the Stanley Cup Finals.

In 1975, Buffalo Sabres forward Jim Lorentz swatted at a bat flying around inside Buffalo Memorial Auditorium before a faceoff during Game 3 of the Finals against Philadelphia. The stick hit the bat and killed it! Lorentz got the nickname "batman" from the **incident**.

Jim Lorentz

A warm day in Buffalo made fog fill the arena during the game, making it even freakier! Buffalo won the game in overtime, 5-4, but lost the series in 6 games.

They once canceled the Finals because of the Spanish flu!

The 1919 Stanley Cup Finals between the Montreal Canadiens and Seattle Metropolitans ended after five games without a winner decided. Both teams won two games each and tied another. Game six was supposed to decide the series, but Montreal didn't have enough healthy players to play!

THE GLOBE, TORONTO, WEDNESDAY, APRIL 2, 1919.

STANLEY CUP OFF; TEAM IN HOSPITAL

STANLEY CUP SERIES IS OFF

Five Canadiens and Manager Are Very Ill With Influenza

EACH TEAM WINS TWICE

...ure, Ber-
...ld

Canadiens, Most of Whom Are in Seattle Hospital

Back row, from left to right—George Kennedy, manager; Pitre, Berlanquette, Couture, McDonald, and trainer.
Front row—Lalonde, O. Cleghorn, Corbeau, Hall and Vezina.

The only other year the Stanley Cup wasn't awarded was during the 2004–2005 season, which wasn't played because of a **lockout**.

Lord Stanley's Cup

FACT 18

The Stanley Cup was named after a real person.

Frederick Arthur Stanley, or Lord Stanley of Preston, was the Governor General of Canada in 1892. He bought a small cup for about $50 at the time and made it a **challenge trophy**. The team that held it would lose it if they lost a challenge.

Frederick Arthur Stanley

In 1893, the Montreal Amateur Athletic Association (MAAA) finished atop the Amateur Hockey Association of Canada standings, winning the Stanley Cup for the first time.

Your name doesn't stay on the Cup forever.

When the bands of silver on the Stanley Cup are full, an old ring is removed and a new, blank one is put on. This makes room for new teams to add their names to the Cup when they win it!

Old rings taken off the Stanley Cup are put in an old bank vault in the Hockey Hall of Fame in Toronto, Ontario, Canada.

There's more than one Stanley Cup!

The original Stanley Cup was found to be too **brittle** by NHL president Clarence Campbell in 1963. A **replica** "Presentation Cup" is given to the winning team, and a third Cup (another replica) is on display at the Hockey Hall of Fame.

The original, too-brittle cup is also on display with the retired bands in the Hall of Fame's bank vault in Toronto.

original Stanley Cup

The Stanley Cup's Rings

BOWL

1926 BAND

1925 ANGLED BAND

1927 BAND

1893 BASE RING

1924 BAND

SHOULDER COLLAR

1909 BASE RING

BAND 1

BAND 2

BANDS REPLACED WITH NEW WINNING TEAMS

BAND 3

BAND 4

The rings on the Stanley Cup can actually come off! It has been redesigned many times over the years.

BAND 5

Trophy Talk

You could write a whole book about the adventures the Stanley Cup has gone on! It's seen the bottom of swimming pools and once got lost in the Ottawa Canal. People even eat or drink out of it! In 1907, the Montreal Wanderers left it at a photographer's home. The photographer's mother was using it as a flowerpot when they came back for it!

Hockey is a great sport, and the Stanley Cup is just part of its fantastically fun history. Every player who wins it gets to spend a day with the big silver trophy. What would you do on your day with the cup?

Each year, the Stanley Cup champions take the Cup on a parade through the winning city. Then the players each get their own day with the Cup later that summer.

29

association: a group of teams playing the same sport

brittle: able to break easily

challenge trophy: an award that is held by a winning team but can be won by another if the holding team loses

composite: made up of many different kinds of matter

expansion team: a team added to an existing league

frozen: made solid by cold

incident: a memorable event

lockout: the stopping of work because of a disagreement between workers and owners

replica: a close copy of something

retire: to stop doing a job because of age or ability

tradition: a practice or way of doing things handed down from the past

trophy: an award given for winning or doing something notable

vulcanize: to treat rubber to make it strong

For More Information

Books

Borth, Teddy. *Hockey: Great Moments, Records, and Facts.* Minneapolis, MN: ABDO Kids, 2015.

Frederick, Shane. *Who's Who of Pro Hockey: A Guide to the Game's Greatest Players.* North Mankato, MN: Capstone Press, 2016.

Nagelhout, Ryan. *The Science of Hockey.* New York, NY: PowerKids Press, 2016.

Websites

Hockey Reference
hockey-reference.com
Find stats and more about your favorite hockey players and teams here.

National Hockey League
NHL.com
Find out more about each NHL team on the league's official site.

USA Hockey
usahockey.com
Learn more about how you can start playing hockey here.

Publisher's note to educators and parents: Our editors have carefully reviewed these websites to ensure that they are suitable for students. Many websites change frequently, however, and we cannot guarantee that a site's future contents will continue to meet our high standards of quality and educational value. Be advised that students should be closely supervised whenever they access the Internet.

Index